www.osha.gov

I0483147

Occupational Safety and Health Act of 1970

"To assure safe and healthful working conditions for working men and women; by authorizing enforcement of the standards developed under the Act; by assisting and encouraging the States in their efforts to assure safe and healthful working conditions; by providing for research, information, education, and training in the field of occupational safety and health."

Ventilation in
Shipyard Employment

Occupational Safety and Health Administration
U.S. Department of Labor

OSHA 3639-04 2013

TABLE OF CONTENTS

Introduction

Working in a shipyard can expose workers to a variety of hazards. One hazard is poor air quality while working in confined or enclosed spaces. Poor air quality can occur as a result of several factors, such as stagnant air where there is insufficient air flow, or the accumulation of air contaminants resulting from a source pollutant (e.g., residual sewage or residual hazardous materials). When such conditions exist, the use of ventilation is necessary to remove contaminants (e.g., fumes, dust or vapors) and provide a healthful and safe working environment.

This document provides employers with the basic principles of ventilation for use in shipbuilding, ship repair and shipbreaking activities. The document includes methods for the selection, installation and use of ventilation equipment to ensure proper air quality in confined and enclosed spaces. For more information consult OSHA standards 29 CFR Part1915, subpart B; OSHA's Shipyard eTool (http://www.osha.gov/SLTC/etools/shipyard/ shiprepair/ confinedspace/ ventilation.html); and OSHA Instruction CPL 02-01-051 – 29 CFR Part 1915, subpart B, Confined and Enclosed Spaces and Other Dangerous Atmospheres in Shipyard Employment, May 20, 2011.

Purpose, Use and Requirements for Ventilation

Ventilation is needed to provide or maintain oxygen and to dilute or remove contaminants such as carbon dioxide, hydrogen sulfide and other toxic or explosive gases. Ventilation is commonly used to supply fresh air to a space in order to refresh the existing atmosphere. Ventilation can also be used for cooling spaces, making them more comfortable for workers while performing their assigned duties. Ventilation can be accomplished through natural or mechanical means. However, this document will focus on the different methods of mechanical ventilation and the proper use of equipment options.

Hazardous air contaminants come from two main sources: (1) contaminants previously contained in the tanks or spaces; and (2) contaminants produced during shipbuilding, ship repair or shipbreaking. Typically, some of these contaminant-generating operations include welding, painting, blasting, or the use of solvents or cleaning products.

Before anyone enters or performs work in a confined or enclosed space, contaminants (liquid residues of hazardous materials) previously contained in the area must be removed. Next, the space must be visually inspected and the atmosphere tested to determine the oxygen content, flammability and toxicity (§§1915.12 and 1915.13). Testing must be conducted by a trained individual, such as a Shipyard Competent Person (SCP) or Certified Marine Chemist, using the appropriate test equipment. If testing determines the space/area to be "Not Safe for Workers," sufficient ventilation must be provided at volumes and flow rates to ensure that:

- Oxygen levels are maintained between 19.5% and 22% by volume (§1915.12(a)(3));
- Flammable vapors or gases are maintained below 10% of the lower explosive limit (LEL) (§1915.12(b)(2)); and
- Concentration of toxics, corrosives, or irritants are maintained within the permissible exposure limit (PEL) and below the immediately dangerous to life and health (IDLH) level (§1915.12(c)(2)).

Even if a space has been determined to be safe for entry, certain operations performed during shipbuilding, ship repair or shipbreaking (e.g., hot work) can create a hazardous atmosphere. As a result of such processes oxygen can be displaced, therefore making spaces oxygen deficient. To maintain safe and healthful conditions for workers, these hazards must be monitored and controlled through whatever means necessary, which includes ventilation.

For operations involving the use of materials containing hazardous substances, such as cleaning solvents, ventilation must be used to remove the vapor at the source and to dilute the concentration of vapors in the space to a safe level (§1915.32(a)(2)). If vapors cannot be diluted to a safe concentration, suitable respiratory protection in accord with the requirements of 29 CFR Part 1915, subpart I must be worn (§1915.32(a)(3)).

While welding, cutting and heating processes are being performed, mechanical ventilation must be of sufficient capacity and positioning to ensure the necessary number of air changes to keep welding fumes and smoke within safe limits (§1915.51(b)(1)(ii)). Appropriate local exhaust ventilation must have freely moveable hoods placed as close as possible to the point of fume generation (§1915.51(b)(1)(iii)).

Several organic coatings, adhesives and resins are often dissolved with highly toxic, flammable and explosive solvents. Sufficient exhaust ventilation must be used when working with such materials to keep the concentration of solvent vapors below 10% of the LEL (§1915.35(b)(1)). A SCP must conduct frequent tests to ascertain the concentration of solvent vapors. For materials that are highly flammable and explosive (having flash points below 80 degrees Fahrenheit), all motors and control equipment must be grounded and designated explosion-proof. In addition, all fans must have nonferrous blades (§1915.35(b)(5)).

Additional precautions to those in §1915.35(b) must be taken in cases when liquid solvents, paint and preservative removers, paints or vehicles, other than those covered by §1915.35(b), are capable of producing a flammable atmosphere under the conditions of use. These safety measures exclude smoking, open flames, arcs and spark-producing equipment from the area. Scrapings and rags soaked with these materials must be kept in a covered metal container. Only explosion proof lights, approved by the Underwriters' Laboratories for use in Class I, Group D atmospheres, or approved as permissible by the Mine Safety and Health Administration or the U.S. Coast Guard, must be used (§1915.36(a)(1) through (a)(4)). Also,

suitable fire extinguishing equipment must be available in the work area and maintained in a ready state (§1915.36(a)(6)).

Even when mechanical ventilation is in use, OSHA requires that workers wear respirators when working with paints and tank coatings mixed with or dissolved in volatile, toxic, or flammable solvents (§1915.35(a)). See §1915.154 for detailed requirements on respiratory protection.

Types of Spaces

When working aboard vessels, many areas require ventilation to maintain safe atmospheric conditions for workers.

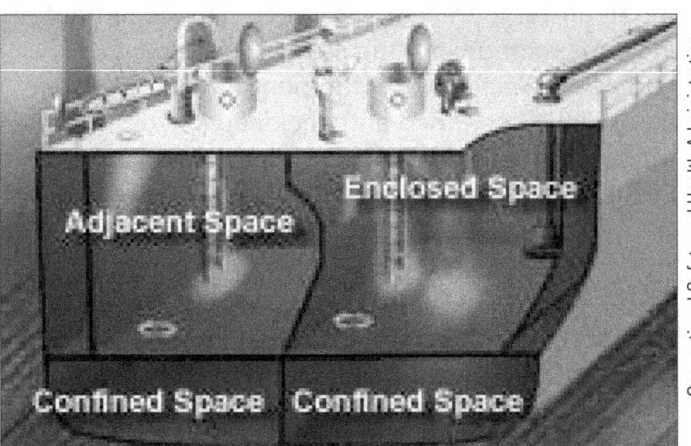

Confined Spaces

A confined space is any space, void, or compartment of small size and with limited access for entry and exit, such as a double bottom tank, cofferdam, or other space that, by its design and confined nature, can quickly create a hazardous atmosphere for workers (§1915.4(p)).

Because confined spaces usually do not have adequate natural ventilation, they may lack sufficient oxygen or contain high concentrations of hazardous fumes, vapors and gases. OSHA standards require adequate mechanical ventilation during hot work in confined spaces (§1915.51(c)), as well as in situations when testing determines that the space/area is "Not Safe for Workers." Worker access to a confined space must be kept clear and should not be blocked by ventilation ducts. However, when sufficient ventilation cannot be obtained without blocking the means of access, air-line respirators as well as a stand-by person must be available (§1915.51(c)(3)).

Enclosed Spaces

An enclosed space is defined as any space, other than a confined space, which is enclosed by bulkheads and an overhead. Examples of enclosed spaces include cargo holds, tanks, quarters, and machinery and boiler spaces (§1915.4(q)). For example, open areas (e.g., large cargo holds or graving docks) may collect heavier-than-air gases, such as acetylene welding gas when there is no air flow.

Adjacent Spaces

An adjacent space borders a confined space in all directions, including all points of contact, corners, diagonals, decks, tank tops and bulkheads (§1915.11(b)). It is important to consider adjacent spaces during work in confined spaces, as gases or vapors may enter from an adjacent space into a work space and contaminate the atmosphere.

Open Spaces or Areas

While ventilation is not routinely required in open spaces or areas, it may be required when working with toxic materials found in paints, metals or coatings where hazardous vapors are released close to workers.

Necessary Steps to Protect Workers

Before entering a confined or enclosed space it is essential that the atmosphere be tested by either an SCP or a Certified Marine Chemist (§1915.12). It is important to test the atmosphere at the top, middle and bottom of each space. Spaces that are irregularly shaped, baffled, or contained within each other require sampling techniques that

include the inspector to enter the space to obtain an accurate reading. Workers required to enter confined or enclosed spaces, and other areas with dangerous atmospheres, must be trained in the dangers they might encounter, procedures for safe entry and work practices, and the use of necessary protective gear (§1915.12(d)).

Types of Ventilation

All industrial ventilation systems, when properly designed and maintained, must provide worker protection. An effective ventilation program is a cornerstone of a protective safety and health program in shipyards. Choosing the proper type of ventilation is critical in effectively protecting workers from hazardous airborne contaminants that are generated by the various hot and cold work operations performed during the construction and repair of vessels. The proper ventilation system may eliminate the need for the use of additional respiratory protective devices.

Ventilation may be achieved by one of two methods: (1) dilution ventilation, or (2) local exhaust ventilation.

Dilution Ventilation

Dilution ventilation can be used to reduce concentrations of flammable and toxic fumes, vapors, or particulates while maintaining sufficient oxygen levels. This type of ventilation involves bringing in clean air (forced air) to dilute the contaminated air and then exhausting the diluted air to the outside via exhaust fans. Examples of dilution ventilation include compressed air, fans, blowers and natural ventilation. It should be noted that this type of ventilation does not eliminate exposure to toxic gases or vapors. The exhausted air should be completely transported to the outside and not recirculated. Dilution ventilation is rarely used in the shipyard industry for the control of atmospheric health hazards. However, dilution ventilation is frequently used for comfort, particularly in shops and other locations. (See Illustrations 3 and 4).

Local Exhaust Ventilation

Local exhaust ventilation is frequently used in the shipbuilding industry and is the recommended method when workers are exposed to hazardous chemicals, when a large amount of dust or welding fumes are generated, or during cold weather when increased heating costs from the use of dilution ventilation is a concern. Local exhaust ventilation involves trapping airborne contaminants at their source before they contaminate the air that is breathed by workers. For welding, cutting and heating processes, this type of ventilation must consist of freely movable hoods placed by the welder or burner as close as possible to where the work is being performed (§1915.51(b)(1)(iii)). Examples of such ventilation include, but are not limited to, electric-ducted fans and blowers, electric non-ducted fans and blowers, and air ejectors operated by compressed air.

Local exhaust ventilation is based on the principle that air moves from an area of high pressure to an area of low pressure. The difference in pressure is created by a fan that draws or sucks air through the ventilation system. A local exhaust system consists of a hood to capture the contaminants, ducts to transport them outside the space, an exhaust fan to move the air, and in some cases air cleaners to remove particulates from the air. (See Illustrations 5, 6, and 7).

Typically, an exhaust hood is placed close to the emission source and the makeup air is located behind the worker so that the contaminated air is drawn away from the worker's breathing zone. This will help to ensure that any contaminants are captured before they can be released into the work area. Most shipyard work is performed in confined spaces and many of these operations produce copious amounts of smoke, fumes and gases. Without controls, these contaminants would build to hazardous levels, affecting many workers. The success of occupational safety and health programs in shipyards very much depends on the proper use and maintenance of local exhaust ventilation systems.

Table 1, below, provides a comparison between dilution and local exhaust ventilation methods, indicating their advantages and disadvantages.

Table 1 — Comparison of Ventilation Systems

DILUTION VENTILATION		LOCAL EXHAUST VENTILATION	
Advantages	Disadvantages	Advantages	Disadvantages
Requires less maintenance.	Does not completely remove contaminants.	Captures contaminant at source and removes it from the workplace.	Requires regular cleaning, inspection and maintenance.
Effective control for small amounts of low toxicity chemicals.	Cannot be used for highly toxic chemicals.	Only choice for highly toxic airborne chemicals.	Ducting style may make it difficult to access the space.
Effective control for flammable or combustible gases or vapors.	Ineffective for dusts or metal fumes or large amounts of gases or vapors.	Can handle all sorts of contaminants including dusts and metal fumes.	
Best ventilation for small dispersed contaminant sources or mobile sources.	Requires large amounts of heated or cooled makeup air.	Requires smaller amount of makeup air since smaller amounts of air are being exhausted.	
	Ineffective for handling surges of gases or vapors or irregular emissions.	Less makeup air is needed to heat or cool.	

Ventilation Used in Flammable Atmospheres

In a space with a flammable atmosphere, the primary uses for ventilation are to remove and lower the concentration of a flammable vapor or gas.

Where exhaust ventilation is used in such atmospheres, electrical equipment must be rated as explosion-proof by a Nationally Recognized Testing Laboratory (NRTL). Also, make sure that supplied air is from a clean source and that the flammable atmosphere is exhausted to safe areas. A SCP may be required to monitor the exhaust area to ensure that the concentrations do not exceed 10% of the LEL. Keep the ducts as short and straight as possible for more efficient air movement.

Determining What Type of Ventilation to Use

The first step in determining what type of ventilation to use is to consider what hazards exist at the worksite. This is a two-step process. First, the confined space must be tested by either a Certified Marine Chemist or an SCP to detect either low- or high-oxygen levels and determine if flammable vapors or toxic gases are present. This assessment, and a review of the work activities that will take place in the space, will determine what type of ventilation to use.

Oxygen-Enriched Atmospheres

Oxygen-enriched atmospheres may be produced by certain chemical reactions, but in shipyard employment they are typically caused by leaking oxygen hoses and torches in confined or enclosed spaces. OSHA defines an oxygen-enriched atmosphere to be any atmosphere where the oxygen content, by volume, is above 22%. Oxygen supports and accelerates the combustion of substances by lowering their flash point. When the oxygen levels in the atmosphere reach this increased level, the potential for fire or explosion is amplified. Where testing determines a space or work area to be oxygen enriched, labeling must be posted that indicates "Not Safe for Workers — Not Safe for Hot Work" (§1915.12(a)). Prior to worker

entry, the space must be ventilated and re-tested. Typically, exhaust ventilation is used where oxygen enrichment occurs, routing ductwork to vent the enriched air outside the skin of the ship to a safe area. See Ventilation Used in Flammable Atmospheres for safe use and placement of ventilation systems.

Oxygen-Deficient Atmospheres

Generally, oxygen-deficient atmospheres are found in confined spaces that have been closed for a while and in which the oxygen has been consumed. This can occur for a variety of reasons, such as rusting, displacement (i.e., heavier-than-air gases) or bacterial decomposition (sewage tanks). Prior to worker entry, the space must be ventilated and retested. Both exhaust- and supplied-air systems will work in this situation. Placing the ductwork as far into the space as possible will help introduce oxygen. However, one must look at the location of the space. If the space is in the interior of the ship, supplied ventilation will push the "bad air" out of the space and into the ship's interior, possibly creating another problem. If using exhaust ventilation, ductwork should be installed to vent the "bad air" outside the skin of the ship to a safe area.

Flammable Atmospheres

Flammable atmospheres can be found in two general situations. The first is upon opening a space where existing product residue could contribute to a flammable atmosphere. Testing is the only way to determine this.

Flammable atmospheres can also be generated by a work process such as spray painting. Both work elements must be considered when choosing the ventilation type. In many cases, an atmosphere that is flammable is also toxic, so when determining what type of ventilation to use, ensure to consider both types of hazards. Generally, exhaust ventilation is used in these cases, but in open areas both types may be used. Supplied ventilation pushes the vapors outside the access, potentially creating another hazard. Unless the ventilation ductwork is placed well within the space, supplied ventilation may take longer to remove the flammable atmosphere.

Exhaust ventilation used in flammable atmospheres must be explosion-proof and needs to be exhausted to a safe area (§1915.13(b)(9)). This area must be monitored to ensure that vapor concentrations do not exceed 10% of the LEL (§1915.13(b)(3)(i)). Placement of the exhaust hose well within the contaminated space will remove the contaminated atmosphere at a faster rate.

Toxic Atmospheres

Toxic atmospheres can result from residues of a product that was previously contained in a space (e.g., fuel or sewage) or from operations such as spray painting, solvent use and certain types of welding. To determine an appropriate ventilation system for toxic atmospheres, the thought process used should be similar to determining the appropriate ventilation for flammable atmospheres with one exception: If the atmosphere is not flammable, then an explosion-proof ventilation system is not needed. However, care must be taken to ensure that the ductwork leads to a safe area and that ventilation discharge areas are tested (§1915.13(b)(7)). This will help to avoid the accumulation of vapors discharged from the space at hazardous concentrations, which can result in workers being exposed to hazardous levels of air contaminants.

Ventilation Ductwork Considerations

The proper installation of ventilation is a cornerstone of an effective ventilation program. If ventilation is provided but not installed properly its effectiveness is greatly reduced. One consideration when installing ventilation is the hose or duct style.

When using mechanical ventilation in either a supplied- or forced-air mode, there are many options for ductwork. Some companies use collapsible tubing that comes in a lay-flat style normally made of polyethylene. This style has three advantages. First, when a worker must enter a space through a manway, the tubing can be flattened for entry without the need to remove it. Second, since it is in a lay-flat style, tubing is light-weight to carry and easy to store. Third, this tubing is inexpensive—and normally is discarded after use. However, this style may only be used

in certain conditions, and has the following disadvantages:

1. Can be used only for supplied ventilation;
2. Is easily ripped or torn;
3. Normally cannot be permitted for hot work since the tubing can melt if hit with slag or sparks and may not be fire retardant;
4. Does not easily conform to sharp bends and can easily become blocked or kinked.

Lay-flat ducting in use

When using exhaust ventilation, the hose must be rigid so that it does not collapse under negative pressure. Most ducting is a spring-wound style made of fire-retardant material. There are several advantages to using this style:

1. Maintains shape, allowing maximum air flow;
2. Is normally fire retardant and can be used for supplied and exhaust ventilation;
3. Adapts well to sharp bends.

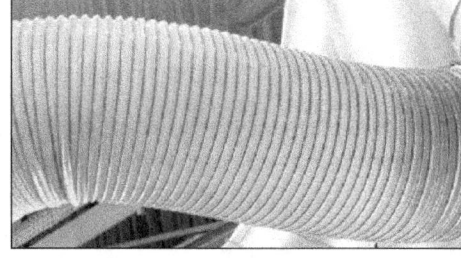

Rigid style ventilation hose

Despite the advantages of using the rigid-type ducting, there is some difficulty in using this style due to its bulky nature and the significant amount of storage space that it requires. However, the main difficulty in using this style is in entering a space through a manway when installed. If there are not two accesses to a space, then the ductwork must be removed to allow for entry and exit, or a saddle must be used. A saddle is a piece of equipment that permits entry through a manway or access without removing ventilation equipment. However, some manways are so small that even when using a saddle the access is still too small to permit entry. In these cases, the ductwork must be removed to allow for entry and exit.

If ventilation ductwork blocks easy access to a confined space then all workers must be provided with airline respirators, and a person must be stationed outside the space to maintain communication and to help in an emergency (§1915.51(c)(3)).

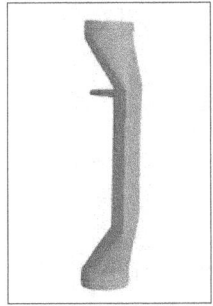 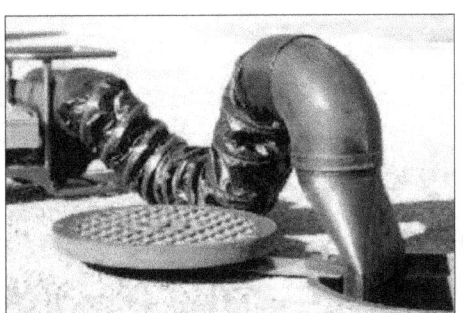 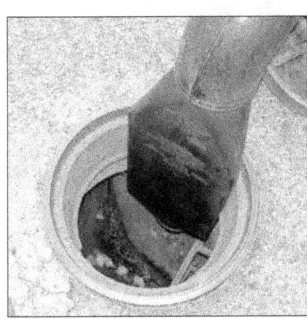 

Photos: Air Systems International — The Saddle Vent®

Examples of ventilation saddles and their use.

Other Considerations for Ventilation

- Make sure that supplied air is from a clean source.
- Make sure that exhausted air is vented to a safe area.
- If ventilation ductwork blocks access to a confined space then all workers must be provided with airline respirators, and a person must be stationed outside the space to maintain communication and to aid in the event of an emergency (§1915.51(c)(3)).
- Hearing protection may be required if exhaust ventilation equipment or air movers create significant noise.

Ventilation Practices — Effective Positioning of Ventilation Equipment

When working in a confined or enclosed space, ventilation is the best means of reducing exposure to airborne contaminants. However, poorly installed or improperly used ventilation can provide little to no protection for workers. Therefore, it is imperative to understand basic ventilation practices that include effective positioning of ventilation equipment.

During the installation and use of a ventilation system, it is important to ensure that short circuiting is not occurring, Short circuiting occurs when only a small portion of the space is ventilated. This occurs most often when a space has only one access opening. Illustrations 1 and 2 show short circuiting in the exhaust and supplied modes.

As shown in Illustrations 1 and 2, the placement of a ventilation system (e.g., air mover) at the tank opening only circulates air in a small area around the tank opening and provides little protection for the worker. To provide adequate ventilation for the worker in the space, the air needs to be directed in close proximity of the worker. Normally this is done by positioning a hose or ductwork in the location where the task is being performed. In addition, it is important to ensure that the ventilation system is moved away from the tank opening (Illustration 3). This permits easier worker access to the space and reduces the chance of reintroducing contaminated air back into the space.

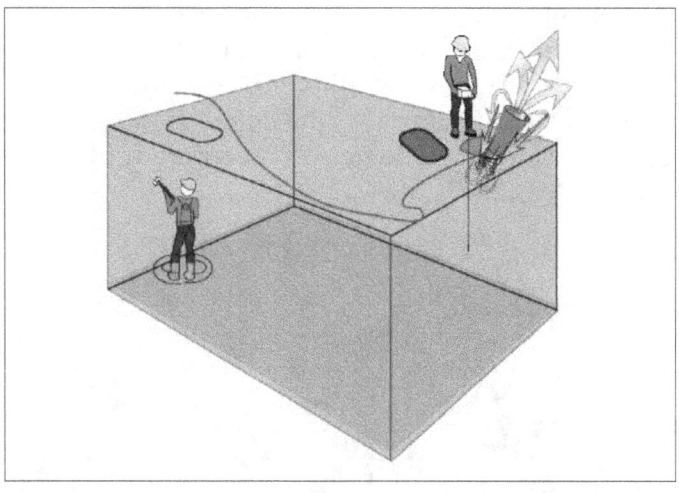

Illustration 1 — Shows **exhaust ventilation** being short-circuited.

Source: Edward J. Willwerth, Atlantic Environmental & Marine Services

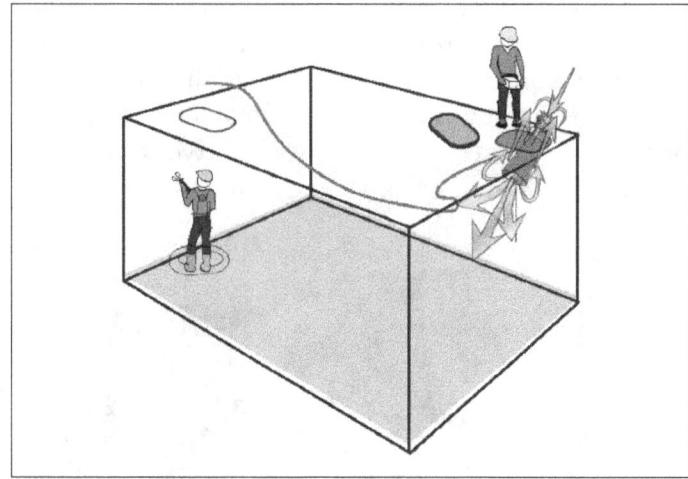

Illustration 2 — Shows supplied ventilation being short-circuited.

Source: Edward J. Willwerth, Atlantic Environmental & Marine Services

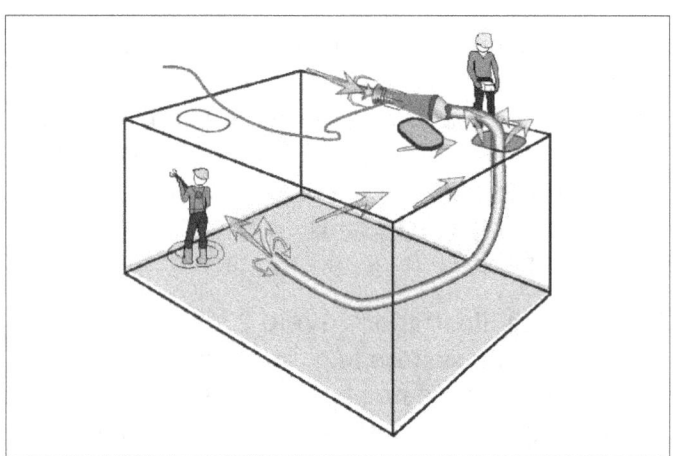

Illustration 3 — Shows efficient method of supplied ventilation (forced air) with system away from tank opening.

Source: Edward J. Willwerth, Atlantic Environmental & Marine Services

If two openings into a space are available (e.g., Illustration 4), opening the second access will greatly enhance air circulation within the space (§1915.76(b)). However, this may not always be an option in shipbuilding, ship repair or shipbreaking situations.

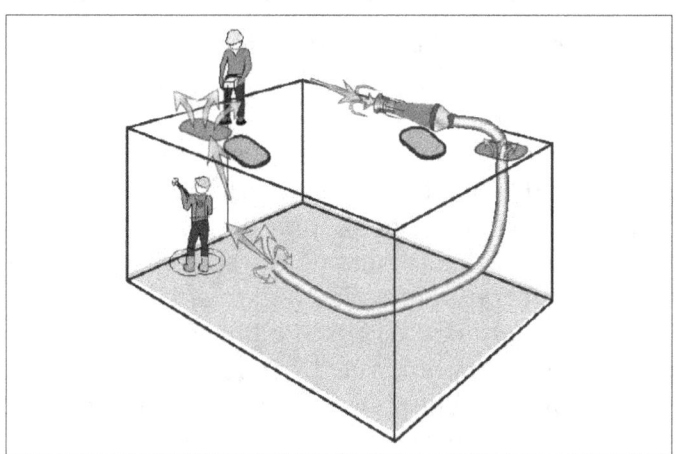

Illustration 4 — Shows enhanced method of supplied ventilation (forced air) when two accesses are available.

Source: Edward J. Willwerth, Atlantic Environmental & Marine Services

Using ventilation in an exhaust mode and placing the ductwork where contaminants are released in the air by the operation is an effective method in capturing the generated contaminants and greatly reduces exposure to workers in a space. Illustration 5 shows this method with one access open, while Illustration 6 shows the same method with two access openings, allowing enhanced removal of contaminants.

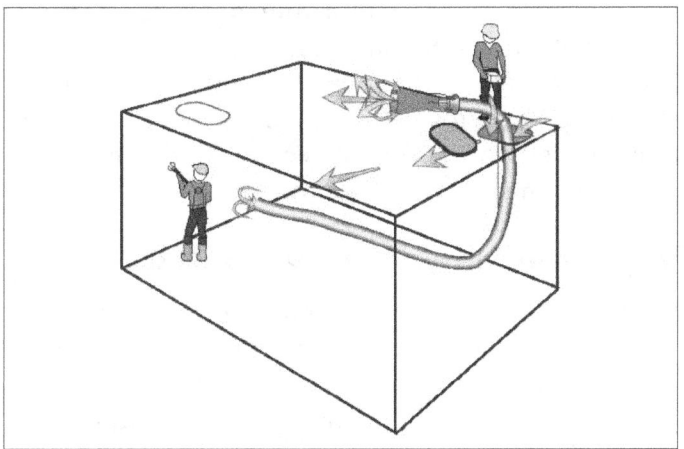

Illustration 5 — Showing an exhaust duct placed in the area where it will capture contaminants, reducing worker exposure.

Source: Edward J. Willwerth, Atlantic Environmental & Marine Services

During welding operations, contaminants generated will be hot and tend to rise. Placing an exhaust duct over the welding operation will capture and remove the greatest amount of contaminants (see Illustration 7).

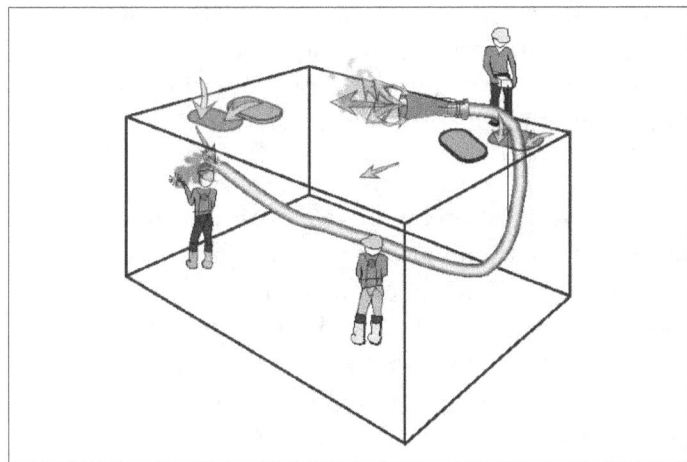

Illustration 7 — Showing the appropriate placement of ducting to remove welding fumes.

Source: Edward J. Willwerth, Atlantic Environmental & Marine Services

When applying paint, the toxic solvents are generally heavier than air and are more effectively removed by placing the exhaust ducting below the operation. Special ventilation requirements for spray painting are found at §1915.35.

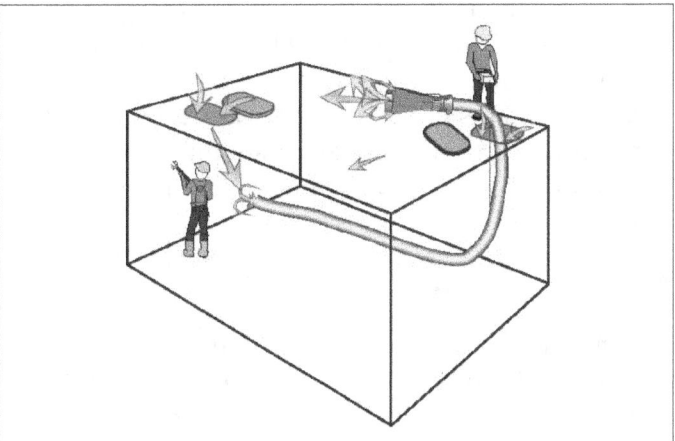

Illustration 6 — Showing enhanced ventilation by opening a second access in addition to exhaust duct placement to capture contaminants.

Source: Edward J. Willwerth, Atlantic Environmental & Marine Services

Further, consideration should be given to the length of the hose or ducting used to ensure the greatest amount of air flow. The hose or ductwork should only be as long as necessary to reach where the work is being performed and contaminates generated. As the length of hose or ductwork increases, the amount of air moved decreases due to frictional losses. Therefore, the shortest length of hose or ductwork should be used.

Equally important is the amount of bends or turns in a hose or ductwork. The greater the number of bends or turns greatly decreases the volume of air moved. Try to keep the hose as straight as possible. While this may not be easy during shipbuilding, ship repair and shipbreaking, keeping this rule in mind will enhance ventilation.

Determining Sufficient Amount of Ventilation

In shipyards, ventilation practices are typically monitored by an SCP. It is the job of the SCP, on behalf of the employer, to ensure that the ventilation used in a shipyard provides volumes and flow rates sufficient to keep the atmosphere within the space safe, and to determine whether or not safe occupational exposure levels may be achieved by ventilation alone. If not, a Certified Marine Chemist or Certified Industrial Hygienist (CIH) must determine additional means for protecting the workers, such as the use of modified engineering controls and/or a recommendation on the appropriate respiratory protection to be worn by workers.

Testing before Entering

Testing the atmosphere of a confined or enclosed workspace before work is performed is the duty of an SCP, and must be conducted as often as necessary while work is being performed in the space (§1915.13(b)(4)). Testing must be performed in the following sequence: oxygen content, flammability, and toxicity (§1915.12).

OSHA requirements under §1915.12(a)(2) specify that if testing indicates an oxygen-deficient or oxygen-enriched atmosphere, ventilation must be provided at volumes and flow rates sufficient to ensure that the oxygen content is maintained at or above 19.5% and below 22.0% by volume. However, ventilation is typically used to maintain an oxygen concentration of 20.9%.

For the flammable gas content in a shipyard workspace, OSHA standards require that ventilation be provided at volumes and flow rates sufficient to ensure that the concentration of flammable vapors is maintained below 10% of the LEL (§1915.12(b)(2)). If feasible, it is best to attempt to eliminate the presence of flammable gases completely (0% of LEL).

If testing finds that a space contains a concentration of a toxic, corrosive or irritant substance that exceeds the PELs or IDLH levels set by OSHA, the space must be labeled "Not Safe for Workers." Then ventilation must be provided at volumes and flow rates sufficient to ensure that air concentrations are maintained within the PEL or below the IDLH for contaminants with no established PEL. The warning label may be removed when the concentration of contaminants is maintained within the allowable levels (§1915.12(c)(2)).

In addition to measuring oxygen content, flammable gases/substances, and toxic gases/substances, an SCP is typically required to enter the space to perform a visual inspection to look for residues, sludge, leaks, physical hazards, or other problems that could harm workers (§1915.12(a)(1)).

Ventilation and Air Change Rates

Ventilation is the primary method used to remove contaminated air from the work environment in a shipyard setting, as well as in many other industrial processes. The effectiveness of a ventilation system is related to its configuration and the air flow volumes that are being supplied and removed from the space. Both local exhaust ventilation at the source and general dilution ventilation are suitable for controlling exposures, but local exhaust ventilation is typically preferred and more effective. As a result of enclosed and confined structures being in close proximity to fuel and cargo tanks, including cascading vents and cargo piping systems, local exhaust ventilation is often the best means of ventilation. This is especially true during confined space entry, tank cleaning and ship repair operations. Local exhaust ventilation can eliminate or greatly minimize the possibility of cross-contamination and/or recirculation of contaminated air throughout nearby tanks and work spaces.

Dilution ventilation involves the reduction of contaminants being generated in the space through the introduction of clean outdoor air. Typically, air is supplied and removed from the space. Sometimes, this can cause a supply and exhaust imbalance that positively or negatively pressurizes the space. Negative pressure results in the prevention of contaminated air from escaping the process, while positive pressure protects products from contaminants outside the process. Despite its benefits, dilution ventilation is often considered inefficient. For example, if an air contaminant has a low exposure limit (or high toxicity) a lot of air is needed to reduce the contaminants.

Historically the introduction of large amounts of "clean" supplied air has been used to dilute existing contaminants while also exhausting air to remove contaminants from the space. Design standards and guidance have defined the ventilation or air change rate as the volume of air needed for proper ventilation based on the size and use of the space. This type of control is often described as a minimum number of air changes per hour (ACH). The specified minimum ACH is the design ventilation rate that must be met, and it often becomes the focus of both design and compliance activities. In practice, stagnant air regions, due to poor design, adversely affect the systems performance.

The determination of a proper ACH for tanks containing fuel, crude oils, slops, sewage or bulk chemicals on vessels is often difficult because of the nature of the products and the varied rate of evaporation or off-gassing. The size, number of manways, hatches, layout and structures, as well as the remaining product residues, scale or sludge left in each tank contribute significantly to this difficulty. These are the primary reasons that OSHA requires an SCP or Certified Marine Chemist to test the space "as often as necessary" to ascertain and maintain safe atmospheric conditions.

Even with excellent mixing, dilution ventilation is limited. This is because to achieve very high removal efficiencies, a substantial number of ACHs are required. In addition, as the desired removal efficiency increases, additional small increments in efficiency require progressively larger increases in the ventilation rate. Table 2, below, shows the required time in minutes for removal efficiencies of 90%, 99%, and 99.9% for a given ventilation rate. In reality, most spaces and ventilation systems do not have perfect mixing, and odd or unusual space shapes increase the difficulty. To compensate, the required time identified in the table is multiplied by the mixing factor ranging from one (ideal) to ten (poor). As a rule of thumb, a mixing factor of three can be assumed for a typical space with 12 ACH and "good air" movement.

Table 2 — Air Changes per Hour (ACH) and Time Required for a Desired Removal Efficiency[1]*

ACH	Minutes Required for a Given Removal Efficiency		
	90%	99%	99.9%
2	69	138	207
6	23	46	69
12	12	23	35
16	9	17	26
24	6	12	17
48	3	6	9

*NOTE: Assuming a mixing factor (K) of 1.0 (perfect mixing), multiply the time required by the actual mixing factor (one for ideal mixing to ten for poor mixing). A mixing factor of three can be assumed for a room with 12 ACH and good air movement.

For example, for a room with 12 ACH that is designed with good air movement (K = 3), it will take 36 (3x12) minutes to remove 90% of the contaminant and over an hour to remove 99%.

Four factors should be considered when using dilution ventilation for protecting worker health: (1) the quantity of contaminant released should be relatively low and uniform; (2) workers should be located far away from the contaminant source; (3) the toxicity of the contaminant must be low; and (4) there is no need to collect the air contaminant.

Unfortunately, the contaminants in the maritime industry are often highly toxic, non-uniform, and non-homogenous, and many are not detectable or are difficult to detect or quantify.

Grounding and Bonding

Static electricity is associated with any ventilation or air moving equipment, and thus can be considered a potential source of ignition in the presence of flammable substances. Grounding and bonding are techniques which can be used to reduce the risk of ignition where ventilation is used in the presence of flammable gases or substances, such as paints, cleaning agents, or other flammable liquids. If the flammable gases

1. Industrial Ventilation: A manual of recommended practice for design, 27th ed. ACGIH, Cincinnati, OH 2010.

in the workspace are below 10% of all applicable LELs, then OSHA does not require use of any bonding or grounding techniques. However, there are stringent requirements that apply where flammable gases are above 10% of applicable LELs. Prior to setting up any ventilation device, an SCP must test the space for its flammability (§1915.12(b)). If the LEL within that space is above 10%, intrinsically safe blowers must be used as well as applicable grounding or bonding (§1915.13(b)(9), (b)(11), and (b)(12)).

The following OSHA standards apply to grounding and bonding when working around highly flammable liquids or gases, such as methane, acetylene, gasoline, acetone, alcohols, solvents, paints or chemicals:

§1915.13(b)(11) — All air moving equipment and its components, including duct work, capable of generating a static electric discharge of sufficient energy to create a source of ignition, must be bonded electrically to the structure of a vessel or vessel section or, in the case of land-side spaces, grounded to prevent an electric discharge in the space.

§1915.13(b)(12) — Fans must have non-sparking blades, and portable air ducts must be of non-sparking materials. All motors and associated control equipment must be properly maintained and grounded. Use only "intrinsically safe" or "explosion-proof type" motors or spaces with LEL greater than 10%.

§1915.35(a)(4) — The metallic parts of air moving devices, including fans, blowers, jet-type air movers, and all duct work must be electrically bonded to the vessel structure.

§1915.35(b)(6) — Use only non-sparking paint buckets, spray guns and tools. Metal parts of paint brushes and rollers must be insulated. Staging must be erected in a manner that ensures it is non-sparking.

§1915.35(b)(7) — Use only explosion-proof lights, approved by the Underwriters' Laboratories for use in Class I, Group D atmospheres, or approved as permissible by the Mine Safety and Health Administration or the U.S. Coast Guard.

§1915.35(b)(8) — A SCP must inspect all power and lighting cables to ensure that the insulation is in excellent condition, free of all cracks and worn spots, that there are no connections within fifty (50) feet of the operation, that lines are not overloaded, and that they are suspended with sufficient slack to prevent undue stress or chafing.

§1915.35(b)(10) — No matches, lighted cigarettes, cigars or pipes, and no cigarette lighters or ferrous articles are permitted in the area where work is being performed.

§1915.35(b)(11) — All solvent drums taken into a compartment must be placed on nonferrous surfaces and must be grounded to the vessel. Metallic contact must be maintained between containers and drums when materials are being transferred from one to another.

§1915.35(b)(12) — Spray guns, paint pots and metallic parts of connecting tubing must be electrically bonded, and the bonded assembly must be grounded to the vessel.

§1915.36(a) — In all cases when liquid solvents, paint and preservative removers, paints or vehicles, other than those covered by 1915.35(b), are capable of producing a flammable atmosphere under the conditions of use, the following precautions must be taken (§1915.36(a)(1) through (a)(5)):

- Smoking, open flames, arcs and spark-producing equipment must be prohibited in the area.
- Ventilation must be provided in sufficient quantities to keep the concentration of vapors below 10% of their lower explosive limit (LEL).

Note: Frequent tests must be made by a SCP to ascertain the concentration.

- Scrapings and rags soaked with these materials must be kept in a covered metal container.
- Use only explosion-proof lights, approved by the Underwriters' Laboratories for use in Class I, Group D atmospheres, or approved as permissible by the Mine Safety and Health Administration or the U.S. Coast Guard.
- A SCP must inspect all power and lighting cables to ensure that the insulation is in excellent condition, free of all cracks and worn spots, that there are no connections within 50 feet of the operation, that lines are not overloaded, and that they are suspended with sufficient slack to prevent undue stress or chafing.

Other Ventilation Requirements

OSHA maritime standards contain detailed requirements for ventilation due to the numerous dangerous operations involved in shipbuilding, ship repair, and shipbreaking activities that include confined space entry, tank cleaning, scaling, surface preparation, spray painting, solvent cleaning, use of powered-equipment and hot work activities such as welding, burning, heating and grinding.

Besides having fuel oils, lubricants, solvents, paints and refrigerants aboard vessels, many ships also carry bulk quantities of cargoes including extremely hazardous chemicals, flammable liquids, solids or gases inside ship's tanks and cargo holds. The nature of the ship structures and compartmentalized cargo holds, deep tanks or shallow double-bottoms often contribute to the difficulty of supplying fresh air and removing flammable or toxic contaminants.

Since ships are constructed mostly of steel, workers constantly face the deadly danger of oxygen deficiency in confined spaces due to the rusting of steel or the corrosion of metals in moist and salty marine environments.

OSHA ventilation requirements contained in 29 CFR Part 1915, when understood and properly applied, adequately protect workers. The following summaries of OSHA standards highlight some of the additional requirements that employers must follow to establish and maintain safe atmospheric conditions within confined and enclosed spaces.

Precautions and the Order of Testing before Entering Confined and Enclosed Spaces and Other Dangerous Atmospheres (§1915.12)

For ship repair operations, the SCP or a Certified Marine Chemist must perform atmospheric testing before workers enter confined and enclosed spaces. The order of testing must be oxygen, flammable gases, toxic vapors, and lastly a visual inspection inside the confined space to detect hazardous residues and physical hazards.

If an oxygen-deficient or oxygen-enriched atmosphere is found, ventilation must be provided at volumes and flow rates sufficient to ensure that the oxygen content is maintained at or above 19.5% and below 22.0% by volume.

Mechanical ventilation must be provided at volumes and flow rates sufficient to ensure that the concentration of flammable vapors is maintained below 10% LEL. If the concentration of flammable vapors or gases is equal to or greater than 10% LEL in the space or an adjacent space where the hot work is to be done, then the space must be labeled "Not Safe for Hot Work" and ventilation must be provided at volumes and flow rates sufficient to ensure that the concentration of flammable vapors or gases is below 10% LEL.

In terms of toxic contaminants, mechanical ventilation must be provided at volumes and flow rates sufficient to ensure that air concentrations are maintained below the permissible exposure limits (PELs) or, in the case of contaminants for which there is no established OSHA PEL, below NIOSH's IDLH. When toxic cleaning solvents are being used in a confined space, either natural ventilation or mechanical exhaust ventilation must be used to remove the vapor at the source and to dilute the concentration of vapors in the working space to a level that is safe for the entire work period.

If a space cannot be ventilated to within or below the PELs or is IDLH, a Certified Marine Chemist or CIH must retest until the space can be certified "Enter with Restrictions" or "Safe for Workers."

Cleaning and Other Cold Work (§1915.13)

During cleaning and other cold work operations in confined spaces, continuous ventilation must be provided at volumes and flow rates sufficient to ensure that the concentration(s) of flammable vapors are maintained below 10% LEL, and toxic, corrosive, or irritant vapors are maintained within the permissible exposure limits and below IDLH levels.

An SCP must test ventilation discharge areas and other areas where discharged vapors may collect to determine if vapors discharged from the spaces being ventilated are accumulating in concentrations hazardous to workers.

All air-moving equipment and its component parts, including duct work, capable of generating a static electric discharge of sufficient energy to create a source of ignition, must be bonded electrically to the structure of a vessel or vessel section or, in the case of land-side spaces, grounded to prevent an electric discharge.

Mechanical Paint Removers (§1915.34)

In a confined space, during mechanical paint removal processes, mechanical exhaust ventilation sufficient to keep the dust concentration to a minimum must be used, or workers must be protected by respiratory protective equipment in accordance with the requirements of subpart I of 29 CFR Part 1915.

Painting (§1915.35)

Sufficient exhaust ventilation must be provided to keep the concentration of solvent vapors below 10% LEL. Frequent tests must be made by a SCP to ascertain the concentration. If the ventilation fails or if the concentration of solvent vapors reaches or exceeds 10% LEL, painting must be stopped and the compartment must be evacuated until the concentration again falls below 10% LEL.

If the concentration does not fall when painting is stopped, additional ventilation to bring the concentration to below 10% LEL must be provided.

Ventilation must be continued after the completion of painting until the space or compartment is gas-free. The final determination as to whether the space or compartment is gas free must be made after the ventilating equipment has been shut off for at least 10 minutes.

Ventilation and Protection in Welding, Cutting and Heating (§1915.51)

Mechanical exhaust ventilation must be provided whenever welding, cutting or heating is performed in a confined space:

- Mechanical ventilation must consist of either general mechanical ventilation systems or local exhaust systems; and
- General mechanical ventilation must be of sufficient capacity and so arranged as to produce the number of air changes necessary to maintain welding fumes and smoke within safe limits.

Local exhaust ventilation must consist of freely movable hoods placed by the welder or burner as close as practicable to the work. This system must be of sufficient capacity and so arranged as to remove fumes and smoke at the source and keep their concentration in the breathing zone within safe limits.

Contaminated air exhausted from a working space must be discharged into the open air or otherwise clear of the source of intake air. All air replacing exhausted air (withdrawn air) must be clean and respirable. Oxygen must not be used for ventilation purposes, comfort cooling, blowing dust or dirt from clothing, or for cleaning the work area.

A means of access must be provided to a confined space and ventilation ducts to this space must be arranged accordingly. When it is necessary for ventilation ducts to pass through space accesses, the ducts must be of such a type and so arranged as to permit free passage of workers for at least two of these means of access.

When sufficient ventilation cannot be obtained without blocking the means of access, workers in the confined space must be protected by airline respirators in accordance with the requirements of §1915.154, and a worker located on the outside of such a confined space must be assigned to maintain communication with those working within it and to aid them in an emergency.

Welding, cutting or heating in any enclosed spaces aboard the vessel involving the metals specified below must be performed with either general mechanical or local exhaust ventilation that ensures workers are not exposed to hazardous levels of fumes:

- Zinc-bearing base or filler metals or metals coated with zinc-bearing materials
- Cadmium-bearing filler materials
- Chromium-bearing metals or metals coated with chromium-bearing materials.

Welding, cutting or heating in any enclosed spaces aboard the vessel involving the metals specified below must be performed with local exhaust ventilation that ensures workers are not exposed to hazardous levels of fumes or employers must protect workers by airline respirators in accord with the requirements of §1915.154:

- Metals containing lead, other than as an impurity, or metals coated with lead-bearing materials
- Cadmium-bearing or cadmium coated base metals
- Metals coated with mercury-bearing metals
- Beryllium-containing base or filler metals.

    Note: Because of its high toxicity, work involving beryllium must be done with both local exhaust ventilation and airline respirators.

Workers performing such operations in the open air must be protected by filter type respirators, and workers performing such operations on beryllium-containing base or filler metals must be protected by airline respirators, in accord with the requirements of §1915.154.

Welding, cutting and heating not involving toxic metals or materials described above may normally be done in open air without mechanical ventilation or respiratory protective equipment, but where, because of unusual physical or atmospheric conditions, an unsafe accumulation of contaminants exists, suitable mechanical ventilation or respiratory protective equipment must be provided.

Internal Combustion Engines, Other than Ship's Equipment (§1915.136)

When internal combustion engines furnished by the employer are used in a fixed position below decks, for such purposes as driving pumps, generators, and blowers, the exhaust must be led to the open air, clear of any ventilation intakes and openings through which it might enter the vessel.

Asbestos (§1915.1001)

In addition to the asbestos requirements specified in section 1915.1001, the employer must use the following control methods to achieve compliance with the time-weighted average (TWA) permissible exposure limit and excursion limit:

- Local exhaust ventilation equipped with High Efficiency Particulate Air (HEPA) filter dust collection systems
- Enclosure or isolation of processes producing asbestos dust
- Ventilation of the regulated area to move contaminated air away from the breathing zone of workers and toward a filtration or collection device equipped with a HEPA filter.

During Class I asbestos operations, OSHA recommends following work practices in Appendix F (Non-mandatory) of **§1915.1001**:

- Portable air ventilation systems installed to provide the negative air pressure and air removal from the enclosure should be equipped with a HEPA filter;
- The number and capacity of units needed to ventilate an enclosure depends on the size of the area to be ventilated;
- The filters for these systems should be designed in such a manner that they can be replaced when the air flow volume is reduced by the build-up of dust in the filtration material; and
- Pressure monitoring devices with alarms and strip chart recorders should be attached to each system to indicate the pressure differential and the loss due to dust buildup on the filter.

Additional Resources

Safety Alert: Ventilation Procedures in Shipyard Employment: https://shipbuilders.org/sites/default/files/Safety%20Alert%20on%20Ventitlation_FINAL.pdf

OSHA Instruction CPL 02-01-051 – 29 CFR Part 1915, Subpart B, Confined and Enclosed Spaces and Other Dangerous Atmospheres in Shipyard Employment, May 20, 2011.

Shipyard Confined Space Ventilation OSHA etools: www.osha.gov/SLTC/etools/shipyard/shiprepair/confinedspace/index_cs.html

OSHA Guidance — Permit-Required Confined Spaces: www.osha.gov/Publications/osha3138.html

Burgess W.A., Ellenbecker M.J., Treitman R.D., Ventilation for Control of the Work Environment, John Wiley and Sons, New York 1989.

McDermott, H.J., Handbook of Ventilation for Contaminant Control, 3rd ed. ACGIH, Cincinnati, OH 2001.

Baturin V.V., Fundamentals of Industrial Ventilation, 3rd ed. Pergamon Press, Oxford 1972.

Industrial Ventilation: A manual of recommended practice for design, 27th ed. ACGIH, Cincinnati, OH 2010.

OSHA Regional Offices

Region I
Boston Regional Office
(CT*, ME, MA, NH, RI, VT*)
JFK Federal Building, Room E340
Boston, MA 02203
(617) 565-9860 (617) 565-9827 Fax

Region II
New York Regional Office
(NJ*, NY*, PR*, VI*)
201 Varick Street, Room 670
New York, NY 10014
(212) 337-2378 (212) 337-2371 Fax

Region III
Philadelphia Regional Office
(DE, DC, MD*, PA, VA*, WV)
The Curtis Center
170 S. Independence Mall West
Suite 740 West
Philadelphia, PA 19106-3309
(215) 861-4900 (215) 861-4904 Fax

Region IV
Atlanta Regional Office
(AL, FL, GA, KY*, MS, NC*, SC*, TN*)
61 Forsyth Street, SW, Room 6T50
Atlanta, GA 30303
(678) 237-0400 (678) 237-0447 Fax

Region V
Chicago Regional Office
(IL*, IN*, MI*, MN*, OH, WI)
230 South Dearborn Street
Room 3244
Chicago, IL 60604
(312) 353-2220 (312) 353-7774 Fax

Region VI
Dallas Regional Office
(AR, LA, NM*, OK, TX)
525 Griffin Street, Room 602
Dallas, TX 75202
(972) 850-4145 (972) 850-4149 Fax
(972) 850-4150 FSO Fax

Region VII
Kansas City Regional Office
(IA*, KS, MO, NE)
Two Pershing Square Building
2300 Main Street, Suite 1010
Kansas City, MO 64108-2416
(816) 283-8745 (816) 283-0547 Fax

Region VIII
Denver Regional Office
(CO, MT, ND, SD, UT*, WY*)
Cesar Chavez Memorial Building
1244 Speer Boulevard, Suite 551
Denver, CO 80204
(720) 264-6550 (720) 264-6585 Fax

Region IX
San Francisco Regional Office
(AZ*, CA*, HI*, NV*, and American Samoa,
Guam and the Northern Mariana Islands)
90 7th Street, Suite 18100
San Francisco, CA 94103
(415) 625-2547 (415) 625-2534 Fax

Region X
Seattle Regional Office
(AK*, ID, OR*, WA*)
300 Fifth Avenue, Suite 1280
Seattle, WA 98104
(206) 757-6700 (206) 757-6705 Fax

* These states and territories operate their own OSHA-approved job safety and health plans and cover state and local government employees as well as private sector employees. The Connecticut, Illinois, New Jersey, New York and Virgin Islands programs cover public employees only. (Private sector workers in these states are covered by Federal OSHA). States with approved programs must have standards that are identical to, or at least as effective as, the Federal OSHA standards.

Note: To get contact information for OSHA area offices, OSHA-approved state plans and OSHA consultation projects, please visit us online at www.osha.gov or call us at 1-800-321-OSHA (6742).

How to Contact OSHA

For questions or to get information or advice, to report an emergency, report a fatality or catastrophe, order publications, sign up for OSHA's e-newsletter *QuickTakes*, or to file a confidential complaint, contact your nearest OSHA office, visit www.osha.gov or call OSHA at 1-800-321-OSHA (6742), TTY 1-877-889-5627.

For assistance, contact us.
We are OSHA. We can help.